Gail Daley
5688 E Sussex Way
Fresno, CA 93727
www.gaildaleysfineart.com

Publisher's Note: This is a work of non-fiction, and any resemblance to any persons living or dead is unintentional and accidental.

Names, characters, places, and incidents are a product of the author's imagination. Locales and public names are sometimes used for atmospheric purposes. Any resemblance to actual people, living or dead, or to businesses, companies, events, institutions, or locales is completely coincidental.

Book Layout ©2017 **BookDesignTemplates.com**

Quantity sales. Special discounts are available on quantity purchases by corporations, associations, and others. For details, contact the "Special Sales Department" at the address above.

Cover Art by Gail Daley's Fine Art. Used with permission

D2D E-book ISBN: 9781536598049
D2D Print Book ISBN: 9781386252641
ASIN: B07JLJNJ1N
ISBN-13: 978-1986618007

INTRODUCTION TO THE INTERNET

THE MODERN ARTIST'S HANDBOOK –Vol 1

GAIL DALEY

ACKNOWLEDGEMENT

I want to thank the Clovis Art Guild for the use of photos from their art shows and their show prospectus.

Disclaimer: *The information in this booklet is for general information purposes only; it is not intended to be tax or legal advice. Each situation is specific; consult your CPA or attorney to discuss your specific legal or tax requirements or questions.*

INDEX

Table of Contents

NUTS & BOLTS GALLERY VS. ON-LINE.

INTRODUCTION

The Modern Artist Handbook was first introduced as a series of pamphlets covering various topics about how to function as an artist in today's ever-changing world. Volume 1, "Functioning as a traditional artist in the internet age" introduces the internet and defines terms particular to the internet and World Wide Web as well as describing some of the pitfalls of going on-line. In selecting these terms and conditions, I assumed whoever is reading this is a novice.

WEB & INTERNET TERMS & DEFINITIONS

A BLOG

Is a website covering a writer's or a group of writers' own experiences, opinions, reflections, etc. Blogs often contain images and links to other websites used by the writer in his/her research. It can also be a single entry or post on a website or social media net. To know the difference between a website and a blog-- consider a web site to be the news section and a blog the editorial section of a newspaper.

CLONE PHISHING

Is a type of phishing attack with a legitimate, and previously delivered, email contains a hidden attachment or link that has had had its content and recipient address(s) taken and used to create an almost identical or cloned email. The attachment or link within the email is replaced with a malicious version and then sent from an email address that seems to come from the original sender.

CLOUD STORAGE Is a means of data storage where digital data can be stored outside of your physical computer. The physical site where the files are stored is owned and managed by a **hosting** company (companies that provide space on a **server** owned or leased for use by clients as well as providing **Internet** connections are called hosts). These cloud storage providers are responsible for keeping the data available and accessible, and the physical environment protected and running. People and organizations buy or lease storage capacity from the providers to store items such as records, documents and photos or videos.

COPYRIGHT
Is a legal right created by the law of a country, granting the creator of an original work exclusive rights to its use and distribution with the intention of empowering the creator (e.g. the photographer who took the photograph, the artist who painted the art or the author of a book) to receive payment for their effort.

A DOMAIN NAME is a description or representation of a computer's location on the Internet. It is usually separated by a dot.

DNS (Domain Name System) is a large database of domain names and their correspondent Internet (IP Addresses) for example: www.widget.com corresponds to its unique number 207.168.6.12

DOWNLOAD is to transfer data from another computer to your computer.

FTP (File Transfer Protocol) is a method of transferring files between two computers on the Internet. To access, upload or download information on a server computer (or a computer that accesses a server computer), FTP software makes the information access or transfer possible.

THE INTERNET is an open network of computers connected (networked).

A HOST is a computer that is used to transfer data on the Internet.

HTML (Hypertext Markup Language) is a coding language used to tell a browser how to place pictures, text, multimedia and links to create a web page. When a user clicks on a link within a web page, that link, which is coded with HTML, links the user to a specific linked web page.

HYPERTEXT is text on a webpage that links to another document or webpage. The hypertext link can be as small as a letter or word, or as big as all the text on the page.

A HOME PAGE is the main or index page of a web site. For example, if a user opens Netscape or Internet Explorer and types the URL, http://www.microsoft.com, that would open the home page.

INTERNIC is the agency that governs and maintains the name and host registration on the Internet. New laws have recently gone into effect that affect the ability of this agency to maintain order on the internet.

IP ADDRESS (Internet Protocol) address is a unique number used to identify a computer on the Internet. If you are connected to the Internet, you must have a unique network number, which is an IP address. An example of an IP address is: 207.168.6.12

JAVA is an object-oriented programming language created by Sun Microsystems Company. It can operate on any type ("virtual machine") of operating system, or computer system (PC, Mac, Solaris, etc.). It is a flexible tool for integrating interactivity and multimedia, and a very secure language, making it a useful language for networking or the Internet.

JAVASCRIPT is a popular scripting language created by Netscape, and is supported by Netscape 2.0 and higher, and Explorer 4.0 and higher. It is primarily used to add interactivity and multimedia to web pages.

JSCRIPT created by Microsoft, like JavaScript, is a scripting language.

LINK MANIPULATION is a term describing the minute changing of a link. Most methods of phishing use some form of small deception intended to make a link in an email (and the spoofed website it leads to) appear to belong to the spoofed organization.

PORT OR DATAPORT a Port is a channel that a server software would listen to, for any inquiries, there are certain standard default channels set for certain server software. A data port is a place on the computer where a wire connection can be plugged in.

PHISHING is the attempt to acquire sensitive information such as usernames, passwords, and credit card details (and sometimes, indirectly, money) by masquerading as a trustworthy entity in an electronic communication. This is usually the first step towards identity theft

A PODCAST is a digital audio or video file or recording usually pre-recorded and able to be downloaded from a website to a media player or computer by a user.

POD OR PRINT ON DEMAND sites refers to websites where a method or printing very small runs of a document or photograph (one to under 50 usually), print, or card as requested. Usually the artist will upload an image that the site keeps on file. When someone wants to order a print, they put in an order for it to the web site. The website will take a commission and pay the artist the remainder of the fee. In this way, the artist avoids having to pay upfront for prints that are not selling.

PAY PER CLICK (PPC), also called Cost Per Click, is a form of internet advertising used to direct traffic to websites. The website owner charges an Advertiser a small fee whenever the ad is clicked up to a certain amount. This charge is defined simply as "the amount spent to get an advertisement viewed".

ROGUE WI-FI (MitM) Attackers set up or compromise free Wi-Fi access-points, and create them to run man-in-the-middle (MitM) attacks, often with tools like sslstrip, to compromise users.

A SERVER is a computer with a software program set up for serving web pages to a user on the same computer or another computer.

UPLOAD is to transfer data from your computer to another computer.

URL A (Uniform Resource Locator) are an address system for web sites. It is a web address used to connect to a remote resource on the world wide web. Before 1983, visiting a host on a network required typing in its IP address. Fortunately, the domain name system was invented to allow numerical IP addresses to be identified with domain names.

THE WORLD WIDE WEB (www) is a collection of information, resources, pictures, sounds, multimedia on the internet that are linked and connected. Using a software product such as Google or Yahoo makes accessing and linking to web pages containing information, easy.

WEB HOSTING is to store and make web pages available and ready for inquiries, or a computer that has a consistent connection to the Internet,

WHAT IS SOCIAL MEDIA?

Social media is a means of on-line communication used by large groups of people to swap information. The number of sites out there has grown exponentially, and the growth is continuing. Sites also wax and wane in popularity according to many factors. The term social Media refers to very large networking websites with hundreds or thousands of members and other online means of communication used by these large groups of people to share information and to foster social and professional contacts. Social Networks or social media sites have changed drastically since I first signed up on Facebook. Some of these changes are for the better some of them are not. If you have joined one of these sites, all I can suggest is that you monitor your settings rigorously because the "host site" who owns the site can arbitrarily change your settings with or without your consent. That is because as the owner, legally they have control.

SOCIAL MEDIA MARKETING is the practice of increasing a website's traffic or notice through social media sites. Social media marketing programs usually center on efforts to create subject matter that attracts attention and encourages users to share it across their own social networks. The resulting electronic word of mouth (eWoM) refers to any statement users share via the Internet (e.g., web sites, social networks, instant messages, news feeds, etc.) about an event, product, service, brand or company.

SPEAR PHISHING is a form of Phishing aimed directly at an individual or company. Attackers may gather personal information about their target from Social Networking sites to increase their likelihood of success. This method accounts for 91% of attacks taking place today.

A TROJAN, is a program that tricks unsuspecting people into executing or downloading software onto their computer. A Trojan may be disguised as anything that will entice a user to click on it, such as an innocent-looking link, a picture or a video player. It can even look like a legitimate link to a site the user is familiar with. Once the user opens a Trojan, malicious software can get to work, often in the computer's background.

VIRAL MARKETING is a marketing strategy that focuses on spreading information and opinions about a product or service from person to person via the Internet or email. When the message spreads from user to user through their networks, it is called "earned media".

A COMPUTER VIRUS OR MALWARE is software created by hackers and intended to damage a computer, mobile device, computer system, or network, or to take partial control over its operation. Sometimes malware is referred to as a virus. There are many different types of Malware. The two most harmful are Trojans and Worms.

According to Wikipedia, "**Malware**, short for **malicious software**, is any software used to interrupt computer operation, collect sensitive information, or gain access to your computer. It can appear in the form of **executable code**, **scripts**, hidden e-mail attachments, etc. It also shows up when you are careless about what web sites you visit. Malware is a general term used to denote to a variety of forms of hostile or invasive software." Malware masquerades under a variety of terms: **computer viruses**, **worms**, **Trojan horses**, **ransomware**, **spyware**, **adware**, **scareware**, and other malevolent names. Home users and organizations to try to safeguard against malware "attacks" by using **anti-virus**, anti-malware, and **firewalls** programs many of which can be bought at your local office supply store. They can also be downloaded directly into your computer from the Internet.

A WEBCAST is the broadcasting of news, music or other amusement using the Internet, particularly the World Wide Web. While the two are very similar, a Podcast has usually been pre-recorded while a webcast is usually a live broadcast.

A WEB SITE is a connected group of pages on the World Wide Web viewed as a single entity and usually supported by one person or organization. Usually a web site is designed to draw attention to a single theme or several closely related topics. A single artist creates a web site to draw attention to his work or to sell his art. An organization such as an art group creates a web site to attract new members and provide information about its activities to current members.

A WORM is a type of malware that reproduces itself (remember the replicators on Stargate Atlantis?). It is not content to infect only your computer--it wants to infect the computers of all your friends. Worms most often use your address book in your email program to send copies of itself to everyone in your address book.

EARNING RESIDUAL INCOME

We may as well admit it: all of us secretly want to not only create fabulous art but also want the public to appreciate it so much they pay us fabulous prices for it. The wonderful thing about making prints of our work is prints are a way to earn residual income on our art. If an artist sells a painting for $500 that is a one-time fee; if that same artist also sells 20 prints for $15 each then they have earned a total of $800 on that same painting. I'm not going to go into the virtues and differences between Limited Edition Reproductions and Unlimited Reproductions; that will be covered in another pamphlet.

Naturally as an artist, you want any reproductions of your art to reflect the quality of the art itself; this means you want to make the best quality reproductions you can find. I have had several artists ask me where they can get good quality prints made at a reasonable price. It's a good question. there are two ways to go with this: make the prints yourself or get them made professionally. The other things you will need besides the printer if you are planning to get prints made of your work is a good camera that will take high-resolution photos (Canon Rebel is excellent). I don't recommend a point-and-shoot camera or your cell phone if you intend to make professional looking reproductions. I would also recommend a good photo-editing program such as Photoshop Elements.

MAKE YOUR OWN: If you make prints yourself, you will need a good quality printer that prints on a variety of paper products. What brand of printer makes the best prints? Well, there are many differing opinions on this having to do with what kind of ink will give you the truest colors, how easy they are to use, whether to use ink jet or laser printers, etc. Making the prints yourself does mean that you are going to be limited as to the size you can make; most home printers will only take legal or letter size paper. The printer that gave me the very best prints I ever made at home was an inexpensive Kodak printer. Unfortunately, it proved too fragile to last long. Epson, Brother and HP all make good machines that will give you good quality paper prints. You can even obtain letter size "canvas paper' for printing, although I wasn't happy with the quality of the prints I made with it. Then there is the cost of the ink. If you make many reproductions, Ink jet refills can be so expensive that you might find it less costly to get your prints made by a print shop. Laser printers also make good quality prints, but a color laser printer and the toner to go with it can be cost prohibitive.

USE AN ON-LINE PROFESSIONAL: The next option is to have your prints made by a professional printer. To do this You will need a high-resolution jpeg or other type of photo of your work to give the printer. If you are not also a photographer, I suggest you arrange to have a professional take the photo to ensure that the photo has no distortions and that the color is true to the original art. You can have the photo transferred to either a jump drive or disc. There is an issue with having your prints made by someone else that doesn't come up with home printing: calibrating their printer to your photos. This has nothing to do with the printer type; even if the print on their computer looks okay, the print may still come out darker or lighter than your art. Always ask for a proof before accepting the print; it may be necessary for you to take your disc or jump drive home so that you can adjust the lighting or color of the photo in order to make the print "true" to the original when using a commercial printer. If you do this, always save the "adjusted" photo as a separate photo and leave the original alone. Making these changes is much easier if you are dealing with a local printer. I am speaking here of commercial printers such as Kinkos or Copy Max's Impress. The photo departments of Costco, Walgreens, Wal-Mart etc. aren't going to give you a professional quality print because their print programs are designed to "flatten or homogenize" color to an "average" standard. If you have vibrant, saturated or delicate shades, you may find your print simply doesn't reflect these qualities.

FIND A PROFESSIONAL IN YOUR AREA: The other option is to find a local professional who specializes in making art prints. Here in Fresno we have several, but Mullins photography is the one most favored by local artists. If you bring in your art, they will make their own scan and reproduce a print that is virtually identical to the original. Ask other local artists in your area where they get their prints made. Be prepared to open your wallet; because of the quality, the initial set up fee will be more expensive than say Kinkos or Impress.

There are also several on-line printers who do an excellent job. These types of printers are often referred to as POD sites. Fine Art

INVITES TO YOUR EVENT

If you are having a show or other event, it is now much easier (and less expensive) to invite customers, friends and family to come and join you at an art show or exhibit without spending hours to do it. Social Media sites like Facebook, Twitter and Local Arts Networks are all user friendly; just click on the "create event" or event button and put in the information requested.

INCLUDE PHOTO: Most of these sites have a place where you can download a photo of your art. The photo should be in jpeg format and no more than 600 pixels at the widest point and about 72 dpi. (Am I talking a foreign language?) Okay, Actual size in inches in your photo editing system should be around 3 x 5 and low-to-medium resolution (some of them even have a "save for web" setting.)

Facebook and Twitter have a way to select anyone you have previously identified as a friend; just click on their photo.

Usually there is a place for a personal message to announce your event. If you are inviting your friends and family, keep it informal; a simple "come out and see my art. I could use your support" should be sufficient. If you are sending this out to customers who have bought from you before, you can say something like "I am presenting a new piece of art on (include your date, time, place etc.). I am inviting you to come as my personal guest". If it is a juried show and you got an award, tell everyone and invite him or her to come and see it. If you are issuing a press release or inviting potential customers, you will need to brag a little about yourself and your art, so they have a reason to come to the show.

DO'S & DONTS

DON'T FOLLOW UP ON-LINE RELEASES! While you should always follow up with the print media after submitting an article, online portals are usually automatic and don't require it: The moment you deposit your article and submit it, it uploads, and you can go back and see your article displayed.

DON'T SUBMIT AFTER THE FACT: Media Outlets aren't usually interested in after-the-fact news. Announcing you have won an award or sending in a list of winners from an art show usually won't be published. Make sure you're not burning or yelling at your reader when you are writing online articles. There is nothing wrong if you want to capitalize but if you're writing in capitals online, it means that you're screaming. Don't put press releases in PDF format. **Don't Send Attachments!** Media people hate getting attachments and won't open them. Do not send attached files until you have permission to do so. You want to send an ordinary, plain old email. No fancy HTML stuff in it.

If you post to your website or Facebook page, don't bury your press releases. Make sure that there's some way to find them from your home page. A menu item titled "Press Releases" works very well. Post your press releases in plain old HTML for easy cut and pasting. The easier you make it to find and use the more likely it will be picked up. Several web sites now feature a "share this" option that will update automatically to Facebook and Twitter.

Get Creative! If you're clever, you can use letters to the editor in trade magazines or the local newspaper to promote your Art-- **FREE**. One way to do this is to combine information about your art or event into a letter with a strong opinion on a related issue or a recent article. You will need to do this without making the letter sound like an obvious attempt at a free ad. Remember also that space is at a premium in print media. Make sure your letter meets the requirements for printing. Our local newspaper for instance won't print anything over 200 words.

HEADLINE WRITING FOR PUBLICITY is an art. You will have one short sentence to grab your target audience's attention. Think about what *you* do when you search on-line. **Tips**: keep it short. Make sure you use your target audience's name in the headline. Remember, there's a lot of article competition out there. Spend some time really thinking about it, even running your final headline by a few people, to get their impression. For example, if your target is art buyers, try to use the term "art buyers" or "home decorators," or "artists," or something like that. Put it right out there. You want a reader to be reading and saying, "Hey, this articles about me, because they just said my name." Tell your readers in the headline what they're going to learn. Don't make them guess. Don't use puns. Don't hide what your article is about. Don't try to be cute. If your headline explains, in a quick shot what a reader's going to get from it, then you are going to be clicked on more than your competitor is.

Most web site builders now have an automatic update feature to several networking sites such as Facebook, Twitter, Pinterest, etc. that you can use to automatically post updates done to your web site. This is a great timesaver.

TRADITIONAL MARKETING METHODS

Does all this electronic marketing mean you should ignore traditional (paper) methods of advertising? No, not at all. However, most of these methods will require hard cash up front and bear in mind that they aren't really interested in an event that has already taken place. Some of them also have time frame deadlines that need to be met to get an article printed.

TELEVISION & RADIO

Using traditional marketing methods, sometimes you can promote an event for free; many TV and radio stations offer Community Affairs sites where you can unload information concerning your event, reception, sale, etc.... It helps if you are promoting Charity as well (10% of your sales will go to something like Valley Children's Hospital, or the SPCA, etc.). Because many of these sites now have their own web sites, you may be able to piggyback your information onto theirs.

USING A "PROFESSIONAL" AGENT

When I first started out, I was thrilled when a company based in AK called me to ask if I wanted to be a part of their web site. For $300, plus a commission on anything sold, they would allow me lifetime privileges, 20 images that I could change (for a fee) periodically. Don't get me wrong, it is a good site with nice features, but it runs over 500 artists, so it is easy to get lost on it. ***Lesson 1:*** *For the price I paid, I could have developed my personal website and had money left over. My Personal website might not get as much traffic, but it would have only my stuff so there was no possibility of me getting lost in the shuffle.*

After about two years, this same web site contacted me with another "*deal*" for $150 they were going to run an ad in International Artist Magazine and did I want to be a part of it? Well, of course I did. Disappointingly, the ad did not contain a single photo of *any* artist's work or artist's name from the site, only the web site name. **Lesson 2:** *if you are going to pay for an ad, get a written guarantee that the ad will advertise your art or website!*

Just like clockwork, two years later, I got another call, and this same website had another "deal". They were going to be a part of a decorator convention in Chicago. Their booth was going to feature a large projection screen to display some of their artists work; afterwards the participating artists would get a DVD with information about their art. This time the cost was about $245. Well, of course I couldn't travel to Chicago, so I never saw the actual booth; the DVD was pretty like the ad they had suckered me for two years ago. It had a lot of stuff about the website, but none of *my* paintings was on it. **Lesson 3:** *For the same price, I could have paid someone to make a power-point presentation with my stuff, which I could have mailed, to every Home and Business Decorator in Fresno County!*

The 4th time the web site called with a "deal" I told the snake oil salesman "thanks, but no thanks". However, I was still looking for a "professional" to help me market my art. In the back of Artists Magazine was an ad for art representatives. This one was costly; for $3,000, they made me 1,500 colored brochures on cardstock, which were sent out to contacts at department stores, catalog companies, and booksellers (of course, they didn't share their contact names, so I couldn't do follow-ups...). It wasn't a bad looking brochure (I got about 50 of them for personal use). However, I did some research later and found out that a 1% return from a directed mail campaign is considered excellent. 1%? In case you didn't major in math, that is 15 responses out of 1,500. Ouch! Lesson: 4 I could have made my own brochure and marketed it locally for a lot less money and I would have had the names of the people it was sent to.

This doesn't mean that these types of marketing should be avoided, but you must use them to your advantage. Promoting yourself as an artist is hard work. Don't expect someone else to look out for your interests. Does this take time away from creating your art or writing? Yes, it does. However, if you don't spend at least 1 hour per week marketing yourself and your work, you will make very few sales unless you are very, very lucky.

.

ALTERNATIVE MARKETING

ALTERNATIVE MARKETING SITES.

The internet has changed how we sell and market our art, how we reach customers and how we are paid. Many sites now feature multiple ways to market your art. These include POD (print on demand) sites where your work can be sold as greeting cards, prints, and even I-Phone covers. Sites such as Dazzle.com, Etsy, and veer offer an artist the opportunity to receive a royalty for the use of their images by customers who are looking for specific images to market their own stuff.

- A SINGULAR CREATION
- ARTIST RISING
- BEHANCE
- CARBONMADE
- DAZZLE
- DEVIANTART
- ETSY

- FINE ART AMERICA
- GALLERY DIRECT· IMAGEKIND
- PAINTING I LOVE· PIVIOT
- RISE ART
- SAATCHI ONLINE
- VEER
- WIX
- ZAZZLE

WEB CASTING & POD CASTING

Web casting or Pod casting is broadcasting over the internet without bothering with standard Television networks. A web cast is the Internet counterpart to a televised broadcast. You are sending live or pre-recorded media out over the internet. This is a great way to advertise your services as an artist. Simply tape yourself painting or giving an art demonstration and send it out over the web. There is a good site to learn to do this called:

http://www.webcasttolearn.com/en/what-webcast-0

54

GET A WEB SITE!

Currently, the internet is an essential tool for Artists. Art buyers will often first check out an artist's website for information before picking up the phone to call directly. A website is also useful because it *should* show how to contact you. Because the general public spends an average of 4 hours online daily, why shouldn't they spend it with your art?

The day is long past also when an artist needed to have a degree in programming and big bucks to set up their web site. Most web hosts now offer user-friendly modules that can be customized to your needs. Many of them also offer tiered price rates depending on what you want your site to do for you. Networking sites like Facebook have also climbed on the bandwagon and are offering members the ability to sell directly from their business Page. Be sure you optimize your site for mobile applications because using cell phones or tablet traffic is one of the fastest growing markets. Most web site builders now have an automatic update feature to sites such as Facebook, Twitter, Pinterest, etc. that you can use to automatically post updates done to your web site. This is a great timesaver.

You should make sure your website is set up in such a way that search engines can get into the inner pages of your site. Having accessed my own personal web site on an I-Pad, I can truly say that it was worth upgrading my site for mobile users. More and more of us are using our smart phones and tablets to surf the internet. The experience of looking at a mobile optimized site versus a traditional web site with a mobile device was eye-opening.

MOBILE OPTIMIZED SITES: With the advent of so many mobile devices, a comparison of the differences between a web site that is accessible to desktop computers versus tables or smart phones is in order. Several web building sites do offer optimization for mobile devices. If you can afford it this is the way to go. It might also be possible to offer an app on your web site for mobile devices. Mobile users get a much better experience when using a mobile site than if they accidentally access a full site. If your site doesn't offer the ability to optimize your site for mobile users, there are a great many sites on the web that will allow you to create your own. You can also pay to have this done for you; shop around on the internet and you will find multiple sites who do this. The best bet is fiverr.com. It's inexpensive and has multiple designers to choose from.

MEDIA KIT OR PRESS CENTER. Just as you create a paper media kit, create an electronic media kit right at your web site under a button called "Media Room" or "Press Center." This is the place reporters stop if they need background or story ideas without having to navigate the entire site. This is a lot less expensive than producing and mailing hundreds of media kits. Printed kits can become outdated very quickly and updating them can be very time-consuming and expensive; it's easier to update electronically. Reporters don't want to have to store big, bulky media kits in their newsrooms. They can simply bookmark your site and return to it when needed.

Have other artists or organizations link to your website. This won't work for competitors of course, but networking comes in handy in this case. If you belong to an art Association, find out if they will exchange links with you. Check out art sites for this also. If you have more than one free web page on multiple sites, link them.

PROMOTE YOUR WEBSITE. The internet is a great promotional tool. The artist or event's URL should be found on all artist or event literature. PR directors who are interviewing or writing press releases should mention the URL or use it as a reference point within a press release. Remember there are now a lot of artist web sites out there. The mere presence of a web site won't drive traffic to it. You need to work constantly to attract potential customers to your site.

QUICK RESPONSE: A QR or Quick Response code is a two-dimensional barcode. These are often used for adding web links to a printed page. When you scan such a QR bar code using a web cam or mobile phone camera, the QR reader application takes you to a Web site, a YouTube video or some other web content. QR codes are an easy way of sending people to a site without having to type a URL. Next to being used for mobile tagging, QR codes can contain other types of information, such as text, phone numbers or an e-mail address. A QR code on a business card can for instance provide an electronic version of the contact information. These were very popular when they first came out. Unfortunately these days you seldom see them.

"GOOGLE" RATINGS"

Let's dispel one myth – you do **NOT** need to submit your site to Google. Despite the phone calls that will start coming in offering to make sure you get on the "search engine front page", search engines find your website on their own as they automatically crawl through the web from one link to another. Your site will be categorized and ranked according to the features that make up the algorithms of Google and the other search engines. A numerical weight is assigned to each component and these components change often.

Here are some basic steps on how to improve your website for Google and the other search engines. Information on Search Engine Optimization (SEO) is often offered as though it is a great mystery better left to (highly paid) experts. There is no big mystery. And if you want to get more deeply into the subject, it's not hard. There is a lot of information on the Internet. There are also many blogs discussing the latest tweak in the Google algorithm. What's an algorithm? Don't know, and don't care since I am not a programmer.

OPTIMIZING YOUR SITE

This is the most important thing you must do. Do your research. I can't say this often enough. **Tips**: think of a key word or phrase that someone looking for your kind of work might use in searching. Ask around to find out what your friends use in looking for your type of art. For example, you may be an impressionistic landscape painter in Sonoma County, California. Two key phrases then might be *California impressionist painting* or, *Sonoma County impressionist painting.* Be as specific and detailed as you can (but they still need to be phrases that a lot of people might use). **Don't** try to search for a very broadly used word such as *Impressionism*. You might also find it worthwhile to buy some of the popular decorator magazines and check out what catch phrases they use in describing the style of decorating that might use your art.

META TAGS. Meta tags help internet browsers to find your website. For example, the keywords Meta tags for **Meta** an art event could be artist, gallery, art reception, art sale, buying art, or anything that has to do with art. Such keywords lead people to websites they may or may not have been looking for and are an effective promotional tool. If you don't know what tags to use, do some research on catch phrases used by your target audience that mesh with your art. Google has a free site for this:

https://adwords.google.com/o/Targeting/Explorer?__c=1000000000&__u=1000000000&ideaRequestType=KEYWORD_IDEAS

Make sure your website is set up in such a way that search engines can get into the inner pages of your site. These are called appropriately landing pages.

It's important to keep your site fresh by adding new images and text on a regular basis. This is vital not just for your visitors who will return if you provide something new to look at, but also for search engines like Google; if a website has not been touched in a while, it will lower its value in search rankings. Most searchers don't look beyond page 3 of a search.

LINK YOUR SITE to as many others as you can. This should include your Facebook Page, Twitter, mobile devices and any other networking sites you use. This will give you a higher ranking in the search engines. My space is ideal for this because you can link every photo of your art that you post to your web site. The goal is to find your site on the 1st 3 pages of any search. People rarely go beyond page 3 when searching. You need to update your information on a regular basis or you will slip down on the search engine indexes.

MULTIPLE DOMAIN NAMES. Submit your pages to Yahoo at http://www.yahoo.com/docs/info/include.html. This is a directory, not a search engine. Make sure your listing doesn't exceed the number of characters allowed, or it will be edited. Most of the networking sites now offer ads that target other users of their own sites on a "pay per click" basis. (The Advertiser {you} pays a certain amount each time someone clicks on your ad). I don't know how useful this is as personally, I tend to ignore these "pop ups" when they come up. I suspect others do the same.

Twitter has a thing called a "hash tag" (#). You put this in front of anything you want paid special attention to on twitter.

If you aren't into DYI, then shop around on the internet for a designer who can do most of this for you.

INTERNET SALES

If you have a web site, you may want to increase your cash flow by selling your original art, prints or other items on the Internet. Most web site developers have a PayPal option that will allow you to set up internet payments. The most common question about Internet Sales is "are on-line sellers required to collect sales tax?" That is not easy to answer because there is no consistent law regarding collecting sales tax on internet sales from state to state, and at present there is a hot debate on whether you can be required to pay sales tax to a state where you have no physical presence. It is safe to say however, that you should check out the rules set up for this in your state. For Artists living in California, even if you sell 100% of your art online from home in a twelve-month period on auction or any other type of internet sites, you are still required to hold a valid **California seller's permit**. Even if you only sell three or more items considered tangible property, you could still be required to have the seller's permit. Internet sales are treated just like sales you make at retail stores or other outlets, through sales representatives, over the telephone, or by mail order. Artists located principally in California should read: **Publication 109 – Internet Sales**.

INTERNET PRESENCE

Do you have an internet presence? If you do, are you getting value for your money? Do you have only one site, or do you use many? I use about 5 – 10 sites regularly and I selected most of them for specific reasons. Why do I put art up on so many sites? Well, frankly, I do it for the same reason Ann Landers syndicates her column in so many different newspapers: so I can get more exposure for individual art pieces. The more widespread your art is throughout the cloud, the more chances it must be seen. This also gives me the experience of looking at the individual sites and seeing what different artists have done with their sites.

Though painful (and expensive!) experience, I learned to analyze each site I use and to check out how much traffic they draw. Some lessons I learned along the way: not to use sites that demand a lot of money up-front, not to depend on the site to promote my work no matter how much I am paying them. Why *not* depend on their marketing if I am paying for it you ask? Well, just economic basics really. Each site is in the business to make money the more artists that use them the more money they make which means I am not their only customer. Although most of these sites have automatic promotions for their artists, it doesn't guarantee you will reach potential buyers.

Reason number one for using multiple sites is exposure, exposure, exposure. Reason two is while most web sites do have some features in common which creates overlap, they are also a way I can increase my google presence by linking them together. Reason number three is that we all have favorite sites where we look for things, so by using several different sites it increases the potential of reaching more prospective customers. Reason four is more problematical: I want to be taken seriously as an artist and one way to do this is to have a business presence, and investing in an internet web site is a lot less expensive that opening an actual gallery. If you want to check and see if you are being taken seriously as an artist, ask yourself if when friends and family talk about your art usually they say you have a hobby. Then ask yourself if your name would be the first one thought of if they are looking for art for their home or business? I will just bet you that it isn't. Sad but true and one way to impress upon customers that you are a "real artist" is to spend money on a business presence

CHOOSING A GALLERY

Choosing a gallery is NOT a matter of taking the first offer you get from a gallery, or taking a recommendation from your Uncle's cousin. It is also not about showing trust in humanity. Choosing a Gallery to represent art can be one of the most important decisions an artist can make. This decision will affect who sees the art, and consequently who buys it. An artist is an equal partner with the Gallery: The artist supplies the product sold and the Gallery in turn supplies the selling venue. Neither party can exist without the other. If an artist chooses poorly, it reflects on both the artist and on the art., Art is a business as well as a creative endeavor. If an artist is pursuing art as a career and not as a hobby artists need to be aware of legal issues that can affect them. Most artists benefit from showing their art at Commercial Galleries (nuts and bolts). Unfortunately, not all commercial galleries are created equal. Some are aboveboard and have excellent reputations and ethics. Others do not.

COMMERCIAL ART GALLERIES or Nuts & Bolts galleries derive their profit from sales of artwork, and thus take great care to select art and artists that they believe will sell and enhance their gallery's reputation. Nuts & Bolts Galleries have physical storefronts and can be reached by walk-in traffic. They spend time and money cultivating collectors. If the artwork sells, the gallery makes a profit and the artist is then paid. It is not unusual for a commercial art gallery to charge a 50% commission on sales. Before entering into partnership with a new gallery, the artist should do what any responsible person would do before entering into a contract: check it out with the local Better Business Bureau and Chamber of Commerce. Ask to speak to other artists who are under contract. Do they make sales? Does the gallery pay on time when a sale is made? Does the gallery make sales of an artist's work and not tell artists about it? What about advertising and publicity, how much does the gallery does and who pays for it? Artists should also attend a few of their receptions or events and see who is attending. If it is mostly other artists under contract, very few sales will be made. A successful commercial gallery will be in a location where there is a high volume of foot traffic and visited by a lot of art fans is ideal. A location such as this may be pricey, but if an audience is already there and primed to visit the gallery with the intent to buy, less can be spent on advertising to drive buyers to see the work.

82

NUTS & BOLTS GALLERY VS. ON-LINE.

Surprisingly there are several on-line and nuts and bolts alternatives for choosing where you will show your art. The words "on-line art gallery" can mean different things, however; an Online Art Gallery will be a website to display and sell art. For example: 1) An on-line art gallery might display art work from their current, future, or past exhibitions, and be set up to promote the exhibition rather than to sell individual artist's work via the website. 2) An artist presenting his/her own gallery, either on his own website and 3) or on a Multi-Artist Site (ArtId, Fine Art America, Etsy, etc.), representing many artists working in different medias and genres. On a multi-artist site the artist either pays a monthly fee or agrees to a commission paid when the work is sold. These galleries are usually non-exclusive and are a risk-free opportunity for the artist to sell art worldwide. Search for them using "original art" or "online art gallery". The advantage of Online

Galleries is that while the art buying public is growing, many people are still intimidated by walk-in commercial Art Galleries. If a potential buyer has access to a wide range of art viewed in the comfort and safety of their own home, they may relax and make a purchase. A lot of artists now have an online Gallery as well as a walk-in commercial Gallery, which means that an artist can present a lot more art to a lot more people.

Beginning artists can be confused by Vanity Galleries because Vanity Galleries are not the only type of gallery that charges a fee to the artist; a **Vanity Gallery** charges artists fees to exhibit their work and makes most of its money from the artists rather than from sales to the public. Some vanity galleries charge a lump sum to arrange an exhibition, while others ask artists to pay regular membership fees and then promise to organize an exhibition with a certain period. Occasionally a vanity gallery will appear to have a selection process because the number of artists on the membership roster cannot exceed the available time slots for shows. Vanity galleries have no incentive to sell art, as they have already been paid by the artist. They are not selective because they don't have to be. Most Professional critics and reviewers tend to avoid them.

COOPERATIVE GALLERIES (sometimes called artist-run initiatives), are galleries operated by groups of artists who pool their resources to staff the gallery, pay for gallery space, exhibits and publicity. Most cooperative galleries carefully jury their members, and most galleries of this type do require membership fees. Sometimes members must share the overhead cost of operating the gallery.

Before joining a gallery or on-line site, it is a good idea to check out their sales record. Talk or e-mail artists using the site and ask their opinion of the gallery.

TO BLOG OR NOT TO BLOG

Why Blog? All the Internet marketers say that creating a blog presenting a wide variety of information of interest to your customers, both about your Art, the art world, your local art community and more is a great way to promote yourself and attract visitors to your website. Also recommended is to create a newsletter, write articles on a variety of issues relating to art collectors, buyers and the local art community, and distribute it through your blog. Report on the latest happenings in the art world. This is a great way to generate daily visitors to your site. Plus frankly, it's a great way to be able to feature your solutions to the issues through links on your site as part of a report. Doesn't this sound wonderful? Unfortunately, my own experience with blogging was not particularly positive. Many of the sites I where I have art also have an automatic link to Facebook and/ or twitter. Whenever I blog, I check the automatic update to these sites which then posts a link to the blog. In this way, I save time spent promoting my work. Doesn't this sound so simple and easy? Well to my sorrow, I found out that Blogging's not as easy as it sounds. Blogging was a little like thinking you can do a major remodel of your house without any construction experience just because you watched some home improvement show! Oh sure, I can write the blogs no problem; however finding a blog site I can use and setting it up turned out to be harder than it looked. Then I discovered each Blog post had to be promoted with the same stuff I was using for my art on my website (SEO, etc.). Way to time intensive when I could be painting! At first, I tried two of the best-publicized blogger sites: Google Blogger and WordPress, and I must confess the Google Blog Tiger ate me. Both Google and Word Press do say you can start out free and then upgrade, which I was in favor of, as I didn't know for sure which site was going to work for me. A year later and after many frustrations and downright silly mistakes, I paid Google the $10/year fee for my domain name and succeeded in losing my entire blog because it disappeared! When I loaded a blog up on Google after the upgrade, it showed if I had the Google Blogger open, but as soon as I closed it, the blog vanished and the message "no longer in use" appeared on the blog site. To the best of my knowledge, any blogs I created there went into LaLa land! I have tried in vain to find the domain name I paid for without success and Google is NO help whatsoever. Google's tutorials are awful, and their help forums never covered what I need. Google has no e-mail contact for customer service, so you can't ask them to do research and find your blog. I tried the search site without luck. The idea of not having a customer service contact seems to be a recurring theme with independent blogs as I encountered the same issues with Word Press.

Unlike google, WordPress seems to have made a few improvements in the customer service section. You still can't talk to an employee, but you can communicate via e-mail with someone knowledgeable.

WWW STANDS FOR WILD WEST WORLD!

Now that you have discovered the ease of internet publicity, internet sales, and computer record keeping (vol 2- The Hard Stuff), it is time to discuss some of the pitfalls of being a member of the Internet Generation. The World Wide Web is the Wild West and your neighborhood sheriffs are rare, so you need to do what first generation settlers did: learn to protect yourself and your computer from the bad guys.

PROTECTING YOURSELF & YOUR WORK

The minute you register a presence on the Internet, you become a target for Scammers. The quantity of email Scams targeting artists has become an epidemic, possibly because Scammers assume that we artists are non-tech savvy. Before you get so excited that someone wants to buy your stuff, take a good hard look at what your new "customer" is asking about. Always check out new "offers" to buy or sell your work before you give them any sensitive information! While nothing is ever foolproof, if you know the signs of a Scam, you will have some protection from their schemes. Here are a few indicators that the inquiry is a Scam:

Previously, it was easier to spot a scam because the scammers were unsophisticated. However some of the tried and true scam methods are still operating and they are easy to spot: The person contacting you may be using poor grammar, punctuation and sentence structure. The person is "away" somewhere, in Haiti, the forest, out to sea, a sailor or an oceanographer—the latest one claims he is on an asteroid (?!?!) The person insists on paying through PayPal but doesn't seem to know how to click on the "Buy Now" button. They ask for your PayPal e-mail, even when the Buy Now button is available. Do *NOT* give them your PayPal address; if they use the Buy Now Button they don't need it! They also want you to ship the same day you get notified by Pay Pal that you have money. This is so the payment doesn't have time to be verified.

PAYMENT FRAUD: If you are foolish enough to accept an offer to buy, these fake buyers might make a fraudulent payment for more than the amount (not possible if they are using the Buy Now button on PayPal) that is why they want your direct e-mail, and they may ask you to send someone, a fake shipping company the extra. You may be asked to wire a transfer of any extra to a fake shipping company (their "own" shipping company) that will come for the pick-up of the item the same day the PayPal payment is received. Usually it reads something like this "Will u be able to wire transfer the remaining fund to the shipping company that will come for the pickup of the item the same day u receive the payment from PayPal?"

Once the fake buyers have verified that you are a viable target, you receive multiple e-mails saying the same thing or similar with the sender's name changed.

The fake buyer asks for unnecessary information, which may already be on the web site, or unnecessary for them to know: Cell Phone or Home Numbers, E-mail addresses, or the *Final* asking price of the artwork. Of course no one wants to lose a potential sale, so I always direct the first (and only the first) contact to my website where they can find any information they need to buy my art. After that I hit the "spam" button on subsequent contacts.

These e-mails are being directed to artists and they are hitting sites catering to multiple artist web sites members, not just single Artist's web sites. Don't give them any information, and don't respond to the e-mail. Treat them like any other inheritance or Lotto winning spam and delete them. No matter how tempting the offer, or how innocent the circumstances, don't fall for the scheme; legitimate buyers will go through proper channels. I was targeted by the guy who claimed he was on an asteroid! How stupid did he think I was? This is the real world, not Star Trek.

Beware of scammers pretending to be government officials: the contact claims he is with the FBI or other "official" government agency. This person even has an approximation of the FBI seal on his e-mail. They think they are *so-o-o* clever! Note: the FBI does not send e-mails to private citizens about cyber Scams, so if you received an e-mail that claims to be from the FBI Director or other top official, it is a Scam. If you get an official looking communication, always check it out. New Scams are started all the time, but there is a site where you can check out the latest efforts **http://www.fbi.gov/scams-safety/e-scams**.

If you suspect you have been the target of a Scam, please go the Internet Crime Complaint Center and file a report. If you receive unsolicited e-mail offers or spam, you can forward the messages to the Federal Trade

DOES YOUR COMPUTER HAVE THE FLU?

A Computer Virus Or Malware is **software** created by hackers and intended to damage a computer, mobile device, computer system, or network, or to take partial control over its operation. Sometimes malware is referred to as a virus. There are many different types of Malware. The two most harmful are Trojans and Worms.

Many internet shoppers are also infrequent users of cyberspace and depend heavily on their internet provider to guard them from Malware or Virus invasions, and a great many of users don't perform computer Maintence on a regular basis. If you are using one of the Internet Browsers such as Firefox or Explorer, they do provide some measure of protection because they use free virus prevention programs to help foil these attacks. Many of the Internet Providers such as Xfinity, Yahoo, Google, U-verse and such also provide this service. You can also purchase virus prevention programs in hard copy and load them from a disc or download directly from the internet. Many times this is simply not enough. Why is it not enough? Because those nasty little gremlins who create these attacks are constantly working to tunnel through whatever protections are on your computer. The war started the second the internet was created, and if you don't want to become a casualty, you need to protect your computer. Most of these insidious Malware and Virus invasions can be stopped short if they are caught early enough. If you own a PC, run two types of anti-Malware/anti-virus scans weekly.

How do you give your computer a flu shot? Well the first step is to make sure your computer security settings on your Control panel are set to make the most of your computer's built in security. Below are five basic steps you can take. If you are using Windows, 1) turn on your windows firewall. A Firewall is software that either checks information coming from your network or internet and blocks or allows access to your computer. 2) Set up a list of approved programs and require that you be asked before new programs download. 3) Set up in your virus protection to be notified if the firewall blocks a program. 4) make sure the programs you use have the latest updates because updates may contain additional protections against Malware that attacks through legit programs. 5) Keep your ant-malware/virus programs updated! To do this make sure your software is set to automatically update new protections. Usually this can be done in the background.

Anti-Malware programs or scans need to be run frequently. I recommend at least once per month, and during the holidays every week. There are three basic types of scans designed to catch malware: A Quick Scan, which is fast and superficial, a Full Scan that goes through every file on your computer and a Boot Scan. The Boot scan is a very powerful tool because it begins scanning during your computer's most vulnerable time when it first starts up because until it is fully loaded, your protection software isn't fully functional.

Even with all these precautions, you might still be successfully invaded by one of these nasty critters. One year we experienced a powerful malware that went through our firewalls like grain through a goose. It locked us out of all our programs. Well if this happens to you, then it is time to call in an expert to scrub and disinfect your computer. Your first step is to turn off your computer and leave it off, don't keep turning it back on in the hopes that the problem will have disappeared! Since you won't be able to access the internet from the infected computer, it is a good idea to have the name and contact information of a computer cleaner on tap. If you don't have time to do this before you are infected, try phoning the store where you purchased your computer or a store that sells them, and ask if they can recommend a company.

There are software programs out there you can buy which are supposed to be able to disinfect your computer, however if you aren't computer savvy to begin with, you may not be able to use them successfully.

MALICE & CRITICISMON ON SOCIAL NETWORKS

If you are a part of the social network world, eventually you are going to have to deal with negative posts. What response do you make when some person posts a negative opinion of you or your work on your website or a social network site? Here are some tips on what you can do about this without starting a major public feud and how to turn a negative into a positive action. Congratulations. You now have a brand-new web site (or blog site). You have spent hours designing it and putting into it everything you think will help you make it popular. Whether you created this site in the hopes of developing an audience for your writing, selling your art, promoting a non-profit organization, business or for some other reason your new site is precious to you and you need to share it with the world at large. There are so many ways to do this beginning with sending e-mails to friends and family, advertising on Facebook, LinkedIn, Twitter, Google AdWords, etc. Most of these sites have suggestions as to how to reach other members to tell them about your new site. After you have followed instructions from these sites to publicize your work, in a couple of days when you call up your site to see if anyone has looked at it, and among the positive comments posted, you discover that someone has written something ugly either about the site, your work or you and posted it on *your* site. This is a little like having someone kick your baby and you are justifiably offended. The question is what you do now.

In answering this I'm going to make a couple of assumptions: 1) you haven't done anything to the negative poster to make them want to embarrass you by publicly posting ugly comments to your site, and 2) this isn't someone you know well because obviously if you were well acquainted with them you wouldn't have sent an invitation in the first place. If you are like me, your first impulse would be to slap back at this person. This is entirely a normal reaction and it is a perfectly understandable, human impulse to strike out at what injures us. However, I urge you not to give in to this impulse. If you start an insult slinging match by posting a nasty response to the negative comment on your site it will only increase the adverse impression of your site with potential customers and visitors that this person has created. It also will make you look unprofessional and detract from your sites message that should be about the work or ideas you have presented there.

You *can* take positive action when this happens, but first you need to make sure it doesn't happen again. Your first action should be to find out a little about who this person is and how they came to visit your site. When you do find out this information, I advise you to resist the itch to retaliate by posting something ugly in return on *their* site. I understand you would like them to know how you felt but this will only escalate matters, so don't do it! Once you know who they are, simply remove the comment from your site and if the site offers this feature, arrange to moderate any future comments posted. If the person posted the comment using Facebook or Twitter, you may need to change those settings also to require comments to have your approval before being posted.

You should realize that if this person received an invitation to view your site the invitation may have come from you, especially if you were innocently following suggestions to increase your circle of influence put out by LinkedIn, Twitter, Facebook or Google. All these sites encourage members to make new connections by checking out other members who are interested in the same things, belong to the same groups, follow the same companies, etc. and send out invitations to connect. These suggestions are not necessarily bad; in fact, you may make some valuable acquaintances and good friends by using them. Please be aware however that the adage about kissing frogs also applies; you may also have unintentionally reached out to some people who practice behavior my mother used to call "rude, crude, and socially unacceptable". You won't be able to screen these folks out ahead of time because this kind of character reference is not posted on their self-created profiles! Hateful people exist, and they just love to spread their discord and repulsive behavior onto others. The positive thing you can do I mentioned? Sometimes it helps to visualize yourself blowing a big, noisy, fat raspberry at this person, and then start a "Do Not Send" list **and check it before you send out invitations to view your work**. Good luck!

ABOUT THE AUTHOR

Gail Daley is a self-taught artist and writer with a background in business. An omnivorous reader, she was inspired by her son, also a writer, to finish some of the incomplete novels she had begun over the years. She is heavily involved in local art groups and fills her time reading, writing, painting in acrylics, and spending time with her husband of 40 plus years. Currently her family is owned by two cats, a mischievous young cat called Mab (after the fairy queen of air and darkness) and a mellow Gray Princess named Moonstone. In the past, the family shared their home with many dogs, cats and a Guinea Pig, all of whom have passed over the rainbow bridge. A recent major surgery on her stomach and a bout with breast cancer has slowed her down a little, but she continues to write and paint.

OTHER BOOKS
BY GAIL DALEY
NON-FICTION

MODERN ARTIST'S HANDBOOK
Introduction To The Internet – Vol 1
The Hard Stuff – Taxes, Licenses & Record
Keeping Vol 2
Framing Art On A Budget – Vol 3
Art Show Basics – Vol 4
Are You Making Money? – Vol 5

FICTION

SPACE COLONY JOURNALS
Options of Survival
Destiny Rising
Tomorrow's Legacy
The Interstellar Jewel Heist
The Designer People
Alien Trails
The Secret Stars
THE PORTAL WORLD TALES
ST. ANTONI SERIES
Warriors of St. Antoni
The Enforcers (ETA* Spring 2020)
MAGI SERIES
Spell Of The Magi
Magi Storm

NOTES